A gold 'coin' of Justinian the Great (527-65).
İstanbul Archaeological Museums

HAGIA SOPHIA

Fatih Cimok

A TURİZM YAYINLARI

Front cover
Detail from the mosaic of the Virgin between Justinian and Constantine.
Late tenth century. Hagia Sophia. Gate of the vestibule

Back cover
Interior of Hagia Sophia from the inner narthex
and through the Imperial Door

Photographs
C. Baykurt, M. E. Çalıkoğlu and T. Aydoğmuş

Graphics
Güzin Sancaklı

Filmset
Ram

Printers
Seçil Ofset

Printed in Turkey
First printing June 1995
Thrid printing May 1997

Publishers
A Turizm Yayınları Ltd. Şti.
Şifa Hamamı Sokak 18, Sultanahmet 34400 İstanbul
Tel: 0 (212) 516 24 97, Fax: 0 (212) 516 41 65

CONTENTS

HISTORICAL BACKGROUND

Tradition has it that the history of the present day city of İstanbul began with a person named Byzas – a wanderer from the town of Megara to the west of Athens – who established a colony on the tip of the promontory on which Topkapı Palace stands today. Before setting sail for unknown lands he had consulted the oracle of Apollo at Delphi as custom required, and was advised to seek out a position opposite 'the Land of the Blind'. When Byzas was about to give up hope of locating this land, he reached the waters where the sea of Marmara, the strait of the Bosphorus and the harbour of the Golden Horn meet, and cast anchor here. To his surprise he saw that some other people, who had travelled here earlier, had already founded a settlement at the place known as Chalcedon (today's Kadıköy) on the Asiatic coast. 'These people' Byzas probably thought 'must have been blind', because they had overlooked the advantages of a city founded on the opposite coast, around the Golden Horn: a landlocked bay penetrating into Europe in the shape of a hunting horn, a harbour deep enough to allow even the largest vessel to dock, free of tides and waves, protected from the north winds and surrounded by perfect fields with fertile soil for viniculture. In addition to this the two little streams of the river Lycus which flowed into the Golden Horn supplied the inlet with the fresh water necessary for shoals of fish. By settling here the advice of the oracle was carried out.

This legendary arrival of the immigrants from Megara is thought to have taken place in about the middle of the seventh century BC. After Byzas, the city would be christened Byzantium and later become the nucleus of the empire to which it would give its name, the Byzantine empire.

From the very beginning of its foundation the history of Byzantium was to be shaped by its geography. It was founded at a place where the ancient trade routes from the Orient crossed those from the Occident. The Bosphorus was a vital strait by which the mercantile civilizations of the Mediterranean and the Aegean reached the Black Sea ports to which trade routes from the East opened. A strong ruler could easily make use of this location and become prosperous.

Until it became the capital of the Roman and eventually the Byzantine empire the city was to live a tumultuous history and witness events such as the arrival of Xenophon and his Ten Thousand, the siege of Philip II of Macedon, and the sack of the Roman Emperor Septimius Severus, and would survive all of them.

THE FIRST HAGIA SOPHIA

About a thousand years after Byzas, another ruler from the West, this time a Latin one, would set his eyes on the same spot as a site for his capital*. However, in addition to geographical factors, military and religious concerns would play a role in his choice.

At the time when Constantine defeated his rival Maxentius at the battle of Milvian Bridge (312) and became the sole ruler of the Western Roman empire, Christianity had already gained sufficient ground in the east and was spreading to the west. Tradition has it that Constantine won his crucial battle with the help of the new religion:... *About midday, when the sun was beginning to decline, he saw with his own eyes a cross of light in the sky above the sun, bearing the inscription Hoc Vince (Conquer by This). That night a vision of Christ appeared to him accompanied by the same sign and commanded him to make a standard in the same shape and carry it before his army.* The cross would secure him victory. The emperor asked his metal workers to manufacture a *labarum* that they would carry in front of the army. A circle of precious metal encrusted with gems was attached to the top of a spear in which the name of Christ would be placed: the Greek letter *chi*, which is pronounced like an *h*, but looks like an *x*, and the *rho*, which is pronounced like an *r*, but looks like *p*. Thus the letters became the cypher of Christ.

Although Constantine the Great is credited with being the founder of the first church of Hagia Sophia, the records show that the first building was constructed in about 350 by his son Constantius II (337-61) and dedicated on February 15th, 360.

* It is said that before deciding on Byzantium, Constantine thought of founding the new capital at Cape Sigeum near Troia.

A soldier carrying the *labarum*

Some sources claim that the construction began during 326, in the reign of Constantine the Great, but its dedication did not take place till the reign of his son. The name of this church was probably *Megale Ekklesia*, or the Great Church. The word *Sophia* (at the beginning without *Hagia*) became popular in the early fifth century, *Sophia* referring to Christ as the Word or the Wisdom of God made flesh. This church was built almost at the same spot on which the second and the third churches would later stand, with its entrance on the west side. The first church is thought to have been, like the other basilican churches and martyriums of the time, a stone building of modest size, with a single nave, four aisles and probably with marble columns, roofed with timber and enclosed within a wall.

The first Hagia Sophia survived the two-year reign of Julian the Apostate (361-63) although in his efforts to revive paganism he demolished many churches. Of Hagia Sophia he is known to have said: *See what a sort of church the Christians have. If I return there from the Persian war, I shall store hay in the centre and turn the aisles into stables for horses. Then I shall see on what their faith rests.* However he did not have time to carry out his threats for he was killed during his Persian expedition.

During the reign of Arcadius (395-408) St John Chrysostom or 'John of the Golden Mouth' who was later to be honoured as one of the four great Greek Doctors of the Eastern Church was brought from Antioch and appointed the patriarch of Constantinople in 398. He was born in Antioch-on-the-Orontes (today's Antakya) and received his early education from the famous pagan philosopher Libanius. After experiencing the ascetic life for some time he had joined the clergy of Antioch. His skill in expounding on the books of the Old and New Testaments – especially the epistles of St Paul – gained him a big reputation. Chrysostom was a very outspoken and tactless reformer. As he had done in his native city Antioch, in Constantinople he denounced the vices and luxury of the rich class, the imperial court and the immorality of the female sex and thus built up a large group of devoted in the capital.

However, his attacks on the misuse of wealth and on other evils made him an unpopular figure with the rich and the clergy. The events which led to the destruction of the first church of Hagia Sophia took place during the reign of Arcadius. Chrysostom was deposed and exiled to Bithynia. During the night of the demonstrations which followed his exile an earthquake happened and frightened the superstitious Empress Eudoxia and thus made her recall and reinstate Chrysostom. On June 9th, 404 only a few weeks after this event Chrysostom delivered from the pulpit of Hagia Sophia another outspoken sermon. This time he was comparing Eudoxia with figures of Christian literature such as Jezebel or Herodias, using a passage in his sermon containing the words: *Again Herodias dances ...again she demands the head of John on a platter.* He was arrested and banished again. During the riots following this event his partisans set fire to Hagia Sophia. The fire was attributed to supernatural origins (probably arson plus flames blown by a strong north wind) and the saint's biographer Palladius wrote

...Then a flame seemed to burst from the centre of the throne on which he used to sit, and climbed to the rood... and crept like a wriggling snake upon the back of the church...

After about a year he was once more exiled – this time for good. He died in Comana, in the remote region of Pontus (September 407), at the age of 60.

ΙΩΑΝΝΗΣ Ο ΧΡΥΣΟΣΤΟΜΟΣ

The Emperor Theodosius I is flanked by his sons Honorius and Arcadius, and the Hippodrome factions. In his right hand he holds a laurel wreath to crown the winner of chariot races. Relief on the base of Obelisk of Theodosius in İstanbul.

Opposite Mosaic of St John Chrysostom, the patriarch of Constantinople at the time that the first Hagia Sophia burned down. First half of the tenth century. Central niche of the base of the north tympanum of Hagia Sophia

THE SECOND HAGIA SOPHIA

The extent of the destruction caused by the fire of 404 is not known. The separate building of the sacrisity or *skeuphylakion* to the east (used as a treasury and for the preparation of the sacred gifts) escaped the fire and has survived to the present day. Theodosius II (408-50) is thought to have begun the construction of the second Hagia Sophia, or an extensive restoration of the first, immediately after he succeeded to the throne. The new church of Hagia Sophia was dedicated on October 10th, 415.

The archaeological evidence brought to light by the excavations and research suggests that the Theodosian reconstruction did not introduce any fundamental changes in architecture. The entrance was by an atrium in the west to which access was gained by a flight of six steps, a monumental colonnade, a row of columns surmounted by a carved architrave and a portico of 2 m width, all of whose ruins can still be seen today. There was probably a narrow narthex between the atrium and the nave and a baptistery. The latter was approximately 20 m wide with twin aisles on each side. Like the first church it must have been timber-roofed otherwise it might have survived the fire of 532.

This Hagia Sophia stood intact for more than a century until the ides of January 532 and the Nika Riots.

Theodosius II was a zealous Christian and ruthless in his treatment of pagans. By the end of his reign he was able to claim that paganism had been extinguished throughout his empire. He prohibited the use of sacred images in mosaic pavements on which people walked; he destroyed the surviving pagan temples systematically and confiscated their property.

NIKA RIOTS

In about the year 500 an imperial vessel brought a peasant boy of 18 years to Constantinople. He was from a small village near Bederiana in the Nish area in Yugoslavia. He was a nephew of Justin, the commander of the palace guardians and future Byzantine emperor. There is no information about the early life of the boy, however in Constantinople his uncle presumably provided him with the best available schools and tutors. It is known that when his formal education was completed he was enrolled in one of the elite corps of the palace guards. His uncle, the Emperor Justin I (518-27) by that time was an old man, who despite being a very good soldier lacked the sophisticated talents of this ambitious nephew. Shortly after, his uncle succeeded Anastasius I (491-518) as the emperor. Sometime before the succession, the young nephew took a new name: Flavius Petrus Sabbatius Justinianus.

In sixth century Constantinople if an imperial personage wanted to climb the ladder of fortune and success he had to associate himself with one of the circus parties, the Blues or the Greens. The original function of the organizations had been to provide charioteers, acrobats and other performers for the games in the Hippodrome. However, in the course of time, they became as strong as today's political parties. Their propaganda could fill or empty the tribunes of the Hippodrome according to their standing with the ruling emperor.

The Greens was the faction of the traders and artisans. The Blues represented the suburban landowners. Justinian chose to attach himself to the Blues, and later it was through the Blues that he would meet his future wife Theodora, who was a supporter of the Green faction. Several months before his uncle's death, on April 4th, 527, he was crowned emperor.

Neither Justinian nor Theodora thought that one day the Blues and the Greens would join each other and start the demonstrations which go down in history as the *Nika** or 'Victory Riots'.

These riots started spontaneously on January 14th, 532, and lasted for five days. During the fifth day Belisarius – commander of the Byzantine army – and Mundus – commander of the Armies in Illyria – arrived. They entered the Hippodrome and killed about 35,000 rioteers – mostly the Greens, thus bringing an abrupt end to the riots. One of the most lively accounts of the events comes from *Count Belisarius* by Robert Graves:

It was not until the fifth day of the riots, which was the eighteenth of January, that Theodora managed to persude Justinian to enter the Hippodrome and make a public appeal for peace. The Hippodrome runs parallel with the Palace, on the slope leading down to the Sea of Marmara. At the northern end are two towers, and stables, chariot-sheds, and offices for the entertainers, and, high up to one

* During the riots the common watchword between the Blues and the Greens was *Nika,* or 'Victory'.

ο οικος

πι γεωργοι

ο αμπ...

Payment of ground rents (above) and labour in a vineyard (below). From a mid-tenth century Byzantine manuscript thought to have been produced in Constantinople. Bibliothèque Nationale, Paris

Following pages Mosaic of Justinian and Theodora. First quarter of the sixth century. San Vitale, Ravenna

side, at the point commanding the best view of the start, the Royal Box surmounted by the gilded horses from Chios. This Box was reached by a private colonnade from the Daphne Palace, skirting St Stephen's Church, so Justinian did not need to risk driving through the public streets. Holding a copy of the Gospels, he appeared in the Royal Box before the packed Hippodrome and began one of those vague paternal exhortations to peace and harmony, combined with vague promises, which are usually effective, after a riot, when popular heat is beginning to cool somewhat and the graver sort of people have begun to reckon up the damages. But it proved perfectly useless, because not backed up by any show of force. Half-hearted cheers came from the Blue benches, interspersed with hisses - but yells of execration from the Greens, who were now in the ascendant again, many deserters having returned to their old allegiance. Stones and other missiles were thrown at the Royal Box, as once in Anastasius' time, and Justinian retired precipitately, the mob streaming out of the Hippodrome in pursuit of him. Thereupon the Thracian-Gothic Guards withdrew from the Palace and joined their fellows in the Brazen House. The mob plundered and burned down the extensive block of Palace buildings adjacent to St Stephen's Church, which was the residence of the eunuchs of the Civil Service.

Now, the least worthless perhaps of Anastasius' worthless nephews, of whom one or other had been expected to succeed to the Throne before Justin seized it, was Hypatius. He had served under Belisarius at Daras, somewhat ingloriously indeed - it was his squadron that had been forced from the trenches on the right wing when the Immortals charged; but it could at least be held of him that his ambitions did not exceed his capacities. As soon as the riots broke out he came modestly to Justinian, with his brother Pompey, and said that the Greens had made approaches to countenance any movement on his behalf, and that to show his loyalty he now put himself at Justinian's disposal. Justinian praised and thanked Hypatius, though unable to understand his frankness in admitting that he had been offered the Throne - unless possibly as an attempt to disarm suspicion and seize the supreme power as soon as a favourable opportunity offered. But after this attack on the Palace, Justinian sent word to him and Pompey, that they must leave at once if they did not wish to be executed as traitors. As soon as dark came, they slipped away, very unwillingly, and managed to enter their houses unnoticed. Unfortunately the news somehow reached the Greens that Hypatius was at large. They surrounded his house, forced it open, and carried him off in triumph to the Square of Constantine. There, at the centre of a tightly packed, screaming crowd, he was duly proclaimed Emperor, and crowned with a golden collar for want of a diadem, though the remainder of the insignia was available, having been plundered from the Palace. Hypatius was genuinely unwillling to accept the Throne; and his wife Mary, a pious Christian, wrung her hands and wailed that he was being taken from her along the road to death. But the Greens were not to be gainsaid...

Theodora entered the Council Chamber uninvited. She was so terrible in her scorn and rage that not only Justinian himself but everyone else present could sooner have died a hundred times than oppose those blazing eyes. She said: 'This is all talk, talk, talk, and as a woman of sense I protest against it, and demand that strong action be taken at once. This is already the sixth day of the disturbances, and each day I have been assured that the matter is well in hand, and that God will provide, and that all possible steps are being taken, and so on and so forth. But nothing has been done yet - only talk, talk, talk. Bishops sent out with frivolous relics. The Gospels flourished in the faces of a great rabble of impious pigs - and then we run away when they grunt and squeal! You seem almost to have decided on flight, Justinian the Great. Very well, then go! But at once, while you still possess a private harbour and boats and sailors and money! If, however, you do go, remember: you will never be able to return to this Palace, and they will hunt you down in the end and put you to a miserable and deserved death. . . . No, gird up your robes and run, for Heaven hates you! I shall remain here and face whatever doom my dignities enjoin upon me.'

Then Mundus and Belisarius put themselves under Theodora's orders - for nobody else seemed inclined to give them any. Justinian was wearing a monk's habit, as if for humility, but rather for a disguise should the Palace be attacked again. He was hard at prayer in the Royal Chapel, his face covered with the coarse brown cowl. At this juncture an unexpected message came from Hypatius to Theodora: 'Noblest of women, since the Emperor suspects me and will do nothing for me, I beg you to trust my loyalty and send soldiers to release me from this predicament.' Theodora thereupon told Belisarius to place himself at the head of the Guards, rescue Hypatius, and bring him back to the Palace. Belisarius summoned the men of his Household who were encamped in the Palace grounds, and Mundus summoned his escort of Herulian Huns. The two forces together did not amount to more than 400 men, for the greater part of Belisarius' people had been lent to the Imperial Forces and were away in Thrace, under the command of Armenian John, enforcing the collection of taxes. Belisarius desired Mundus to take his Huns round by the winding alley called 'The Snail' to the Gate of Death, at the south-east of the Hippodrome, through which the dead bodies of gladiators had formerly been dragged. He was to wait there for orders. Then Belisarius himself rode with his people through the Palace grounds to the end of the High Street, where the Senate House is, and turned left to the gates of the Brazen House. Finding no sentry outside and the gates still shut, he rapped with the pommel of his sword and shouted: 'I am Belisarius, Commander of the Armies in the East. Open in the name of his Sacred Majesty, the Emperor Justinian!' But no answer came. The soldiers preferred, like the Senate, to wait on events. The gates were of massive brass and not easily forced, so after a second summons he went back to the Palace and reported to Theodora that the Guards were not available. She told him that he must do what he could with the few men at his disposal.

He decided to go past St Stephen's Church, now also burned, and straight up to the Royal Box. To do so he must pass through the ruins of the Eunuchs' Residence, which were still smouldering. Every now and then a wall would collapse or a sudden fire blaze up again. The horses were terrified by the smoke, and would not face it, so he gave the order to dismount and sent them back. Wetting their cloaks and wrapping them about their faces, his people rushed across in two and threes and reached the Blue Colonnade of the Hippodrome (it is ornamented with sheer lapis-lazuli) which mounts gradually to the Royal Box. But they found the door at the end barred and guarded. It was dangerous to force it: that would mean fighting a way in darkness up a narrow staircase, while perhaps a crowd of Greens was sent round to attack them in the rear. Belisarius gave the order to turn about. This time he led his people along to the main entrance of the Hippodrome, on the northern side, between the towers.

. . . the Demarch and Democrat of the Greens both made boastful speeches, while the Blues present sat in glum silence. It was now plain that the Greens had succeeded in appointing an Emperor of their own colour; and the Blue Demarch bitterly repented having made that truce with them. Then suddenly a cry arose and Belisarius was seen marching into the Hippodrome, with his sword drawn, at the head of his mailclad soldiers. He turned and called out to Hypatius as he sat in the Box above him: 'Illustrious Hypatius, it is the Emperor's seat that you have taken; and you have no right to occupy it. His orders are that you return at once to the Palace and place yourself at his disposal.'

To the general surprise (for only the leading factionists were aware how unwilling a monarch he was), Hypatius rose obediently and moved towards the door of the Box; but the Demarch of the Greens, who was seated near him, roughly forced him back into his chair. Then a crowd of Greens began to threaten Belisarius's men. He charged along the benches at them. They yelled and scrambled back in disorder. They were only a mob of city loafers, and their weapons were adapted for murder, not for fighting; moreover, they wore no armour. So Belisarius' 200 men, fully armoured, were fully a match for their thousands. Meanwhile Mundus, waiting outside the Gate of Death, heard the roar of alarm from within, and realized that Belisarius' people were engaged. He charged in with his Huns against the Greens, who were leaping over the barriers into the arena, and slaughtered them in droves. Some of them tried to take refuge on the pedestals of the statues ranged along the central barrier - that of the Emperor Theodosius with the napkin in his hand, and the three great twisted serpents, brought from Delphi, which once supported the priestess's tripod there and the statues of famous charioteers, including one of my former master Damocles which Theodora had recently erected there, but these fugitives were soon pulled down and killed. Then the Blues, who were all seated together as usual, joined in the fight. Led by two of Justinian's own nephews, they made a rush for the Royal Box and, after a severe struggle, killed the Green Demarch and his men, secured Hypatius and Pompey and handed them over to Rufinus, who was assisting Belisarius. Rufinus conducted them to the Palace by way of the narrow staircase and the Blue Colonnade.

The Greens had now recovered from their surprise and began to fight desperately. Belisarius and Mundus were forced to go on killing methodically until once more the silk-clad simpletons with their billowing sleeves and their long, pomaded hair retreated in panic. At last Belisarius was able to withdraw some of his men peaceably to the North Gate and send some others to guard the remaining gates; and Mundus also called off his Huns. But there was no holding back the Blues, who would now be satisfied only with a total extermination of the Greens. Belisarius and Mundus did not think it wise to interfere: they stood and grimly watched the fratricidal slaughter, as one might watch a battle between cranes and pygmies - with sympathies somewhat perhaps inclined to the side of the pygmies, who were almost as inhuman as the cranes, though not less grotesque in appearance. When it was clear that the Blues had won a handsome victory (in the names of the double-natured Son of his Vice-regent, the double-dealing Emperor), Belisarius returned to the Palace for further orders, and Mundus with him. Soon my mistress was embracing her dear husband, all bespattered with blood as he was. But a whole horde of Blues from the suburbs, where the Colour was very strong, now came running up with all sorts of weapons and burst into the Hippodrome to assist in the massacre. They had been armed at the Arsenal by Narses, who had bribed the Democrat of the Blues to call for volunteers against the usurping Hypatius. They were followed by the Guards from the Brazen House, equally eager now to show their loyalty to Justinian by a butchery of the Greens.

Thirty-five thousand Greens and a few hundred Blues were killed outright before the day ended, and a great many more were severely wounded. The crowd had also attacked the Green stables - killing grooms, and hamstringing the horses and burning chariots. Then began a furious hunt for unrepentant Greens through the City, and by the next morning there was not a man or woman left who was still wearing the hated favour… Thus ended the so-called Victory Riots, and with them, for a time at least, the feud between Greens and Blues. The Greens were utterly broken, and Justinian stabilized this happy state of affairs by putting an end by edict to all chariot-racing in the City. However, it was revived again a few years later; so the Green faction was bound to be revived too. The Blues could not, after all, compete against themselves. In a few years' time the Greens had become as rowdy as ever, gathering together under the protection of their Colour all elements in the City hostile to the Emperor and to the Orthodox Faith; and once more there were murder-gangs abroad at dusk.

Opposite Hagia Sophia after it became a mosque and Sultan Ahmet square

The Emperor Justinian supervising the construction of the third Hagia Sophia. Manuscript from the *Chronicle of Manasses*. Fourteenth century. Biblioteca Vaticana, Rome

THE THIRD HAGIA SOPHIA

The construction of the third Hagia Sophia started immediately after the dead bodies were carted away and the debris of the fire was removed from the area on February 23rd 532 and lasted until December 27th, 537, the day when the new edifice was dedicated. The church from this date on, until the city fell to the Turks on May 29th, 1453 would be used for great state and church occasions such as coronations, triumphs, weddings of the emperor, and the synods. The accomplishment of such a work in about six years – if one keeps in mind that the Cathedral of Notre Dame in Chartres was completed in about 30 years and St Paul's in London in 95 years – indicates that its planning must have begun a long time before the construction started.

One of the anonymous sources, *Diegesis* (Narration), thought to date from the ninth century, has a colourful history of this third edifice and it reads that

…two teams of five thousand workmen, each team under fifty masters, building the two sides of the church in competition with one another: the plan of the church was revealed to the emperor by an angel; a special mortar was made with a broth of barley and the bark of elm for the foundation; special bricks – which were twelve times lighter than those ever produced before – made in Rhodes for the dome; relics of saints were placed between every group of twelve bricks and the construction work was accompanied by prayers…

Men of Constantinople praying in the church of Hagia Sophia. Miniature from *Skylitzes Chronicle*. Twelfth century. Biblioteca Nacional, Madrid

Legends about the original sites of the columns used have lingered to the present day. Some maintain that the monolithic verd antique columns which are mostly placed on either side of the nave, were brought from the temple of Artemis, which was one of the Seven Wonders of the ancient world, near Ephesus. It is probable that the story derives from the fact that the Byzantines thought that columns of such size could have only been brought from an important monument. In fact these columns came from the marble quarries in Thessally. The Theban porphyry columns which are placed in pairs in the exedrae, are said to have come from the temple that Aurelian had built in Rome, modelled after the temple of the Sun at Baalbek. These columns must have been re-used material because porphyry was no longer quarried in the sixth century Byzantine empire.

The task of constructing the new church was given to Anthemius of Tralles (today's Aydın in western Turkey), and the elder Isidorus of Miletus. It is surprising that there is no information about any other building either of these architects built. In the ancient sources they are referred to not as architects but engineers (*mechanapoioi*), in the sense of those who teach and profess various arts and designs and know how to bring new solutions to problems.

Byzantine architects had been familiar with the construction of domes, but a dome of approximately 33 m in diameter that was not resting on solid walls had not been built before. Until that time a building of even half of Hagia Sophia's size had

The dome of Hagia Sophia hovers some 56 m above the floor. Its present day west-east diameter is about 31.8 m and the other is 30.9 m. The capital suffered a number of earthquakes in the middle of the sixth century and a part of the dome, the semidome in the east and its arch collapsed in May 7, 558. At the time the city was captured by the Turks the dome was occupied by a figure of the Pantokrator which stood open until 1609 when it was covered by the order of Ahmet I. (The four seraphim on the pendentives were spared). The Koranic inscription at centre of the dome is thought to have been added in the eighteenth century (renewed in the mid-nineteenth century) and it reads in Arabic

In the name of God the merciful and pitiful, God is the light of heaven and earth. His light is Himself, not as that which shines through glass or gleams in the morning star, or glows in the firebrand. Referring to Allah as the light of heaven and earth, it echoes the inscription in the mosaic of the lunette of the Imperial Door.

not been constructed, and it has been suggested that no architect of the time could have calculated the thrust that would be generated by a masonry dome of that size. The application of a dome of such size on a square bay and the use of half-domes and pendentives – as often mistakenly thought their use was not something revolutionary – confirm the talents and courage of the two architects.

The outer appearance of the building gives the impression that the early Byzantines did not give great importance to the exterior of their churches, and reserved the splendour for the interior. The mortar which covered its fine naked brickwork has also increased its bulky appearance. Nevertheless, owing to this mortar which protected them from exposure to the air, the walls have reached the present in good condition.

Historical sources claim that the original dome was some 7 m lower than the present one.

The historian Procopius in his work titled *De aedificiis* (Buildings) gives a detailed account of the building activities of Justinian the Great. However, Procopius is not very reliable on details. Nevertheless, it is understood that the building began deforming while it was being built. When the dome base was reached, the space to be roofed had expanded beyond the original estimate. Although it was eventually built, this dome was not to survive more than 20 years.

On December 14th, 557, the building was shaken by an earthquake, and on May 7th, 558 parts of the eastern arch and semidome and dome fell. The Byzantine historian Agathias relates that

... Through the earthquake the church had lost the most central portion of its roof, that part which is higher than the rest. The emperor restored it, strengthened it and gave it greater height. Although Anthemius was then dead, Isidorus the younger and other architects considered the previous design, and by that which remained they judged of what had fallen, made out its structure and its weakness. At the east and west they left the great arches in place as they had been. At the north and south they took the construction on the curve and caused it to project inward more, making it gently wider to correspond better to the others and make the equilateral harmony more perfect thus reducing the distortion of the void, stealing off a little of its extent to make the plan rectangular. Then they rebuilt the crowning middle part - orb, hemisphere, or what you will - and this became more nearly perfect, well turned, and everywhere true to line, narrower and steep in profile...

The failure of the first dome was caused by the inadequacy of lateral supports. This shortcoming must have been realised by the architects of the first dome because four great exterior buttresses were built up to the level of the dome base.

On October 26th, 989 13 out of the 40 ribs fell down and it had to repaired by the Armenian architect Trdat of Ani. On May 26th, 1362 another 13 ribs fell down. This time the restoration was carried out by an architect named Astras and the Italian Giovanni Peralta. The repair work of the monument continued after the Turkish conquest, the major repairs being carried out in 1847-49 by the Swiss architects Gaspare and Guiseppe Fossati.

Although the present edifice on the whole is the one erected by Justinian, its original furnishings did not survive. It is known that in the apse of the church there was a *synthronon* of seven steps for the clergy to sit on. In front of the *synthronon* rose a splendid *ciborium* with a pyramidal roof sheltering the altar.

The marble used in the arcading, in the columns of the gallery aisle, some of the pillars of the ground floor and the floor of the building itself, the frames of the doors and windows and parts of the wall surfaces, all came from the island of Proconnesus (today's Marmara island) in the Sea of Marmara. The capitals are of

the same marble, deeply carved and on their middle sections is a monogram which when deciphered gives the names of Justinian and Theodora and the titles 'Basileus' and 'Augusta'. Acanthus leaves bend from the two sides towards the monogram as if they are blown by a strong wind. The arches above the capitals are decorated with non-figured mosaics.

Diegesis narrates that during the dedication ceremony on December 27th, 537 Justinian exclaimed 'I have vanquished thee, Solomon!' The spot which is known as the 'Coronation Square' probably came to be used for this purpose during the last centuries of the empire. Justinian and his successors probably preferred to use a screened area between the pier and the columns closest to this spot. This area would have had direct access from outside, protected the emperor from the public gaze and also would be close to the ambo and sanctuary. Traces of the screen columns are still visible on the floor. The later coronation spot is decorated with discs of granite, green and red porphyry, verd antique and other kinds of stone.

Tradition has it that the centre of this pavement where the feet of the Byzantine emperor touched was in the past regarded as the centre of the world. This is not very surprising, because the Byzantine emperors genuinely believed that they had a divine mission on earth. Among the variety of things they did to express this belief was the wearing of high-heeled shoes to look taller than the rest of the people. They took this to such an extent that they bowed down so that their heads would not hit the lintel while passing through the gate of the nave of the present building.

During the Byzantine period the social status of a person was judged by the number and colour of silk costumes he was allowed to own, permission being granted by the court. The colour they liked most was the purple obtained from a kind of shellfish called *murex trunculus*. The Byzantine emperors called themselves *Porphyrogenitus* or 'Born in the Purple' which was the most prestigious title. This was not a fancy, for the babies of the imperial family were really born in a room where the walls, curtains, carpets and everything was purple. It is said that they even signed their names in purple ink. During the Nika riots when Justinian wanted to flee from Constantinople, his wife Theodora said 'The purple is the best winding-sheet!'

Opposite Hagia Sophia. The dome and eastern semi-dome

Shallow relief decoration showing the dove of the Holy Spirit poised above the top of a throne, on which rests the Gospel of Saint John. Detail from the cornice of the Imperial Door to the nave in Hagia Sophia.

Detail from the bronze door of the vestibule in Hagia Sophia. This bronze door is thought to date from the second century BC and it came from another monument. It is very richly decorated and at present because of the raising of the floor its two halves are kept permanently open. Each half has two recessed panels bordered with several bands of rinceaux of different widths and a band of studded meander. In each recessed panel a ninth-century circled monogram with crosses is set.

Opposite Hagia Sophia. Interior from the south-western exedra

CRUSADERS IN CONSTANTINOPLE

After he had been in office a short time Pope Innocent III (reigned 1198-1216) began to preach about the Fourth Crusade. He wrote letters throughout the Christian world and ordered bishops to send forces or cash donations for this venture. The French courts were the first to participate. Count Thibault of Champagne, Louis of Blois, Reynald of Montmirail, Count Baldwin of Flanders and his brother Henry were among the nobles who answered his appeal. During the negotiations in Venice, the Doge Henricus Dandolo offered them *transports to carry 4,500 horses and 9,000 squires, and ships for 4,500 knights and 20,000 sergeants on foot* totalling 85,000 marks* worth. In addition he suggested *fifty armed galleys* free of charge for the half of the booty.

Beginning with their departure from Venice the initiation of the Fourth Crusade was directed by Henricus Dandolo. First, despite the protests of the Pope and some of the knights, the Christian city of Zara (Zadar) on the Adriatic coast was captured from the Hungarians and looted. It was in Zara that the Fourth Crusade found itself involved in the intrigues of the royal family of the Byzantine Empire, events which eventually led them to Constantinople in the summer of 1203.

Geoffroy de Villehardouin**, who compiled a history of the Fourth Crusade in which he had participated, leaves a vivid picture of the events that took place during the fall of Constantinople

. . . On the Friday morning the warships, galleys, and other vessels approached the city in due order, and began to deliver a fierce and determined assault. In many places the Crusaders landed and advanced right up to the walls; in many others the scaling ladders on the ships came so close to the battlements that those on the walls and the towers crossed lances hand to hand with their assailants. The assault continued, fast and fierce and furious, in more than a hundred places, till round about three o'clock in the afternoon.

But, for our sins, our troops were repulsed in that attack, and those that had landed from the galleys and transports were forcibly driven back aboard. I must admit that on that day our army lost more men than the Greeks, and the latter were greatly delighted. Some of our people withdrew from the assault, taking their ships right out of the battle; others let their vessels ride at anchor so near the walls of the city that each side was able to launch stones from petraries and mangonels at the other.

* Not a coin, but a denomination in weight of gold or silver
** Geoffroy de Villehardouin was the son of a French nobleman from the Champagne country. His book is regarded as the most reliable source on the subject. He was unable to return home, and died in about 1218, in Romania.

Opposite Hagia Sophia. The Imperial Door from the interior

Affin quil ne seble
que par enuie
ennuy ou faulte
dauoir assez veu
liistoire doultre mer Ie naye de
laisse la conqueste de consta
tinoplé faicte par les francois
Ie la toucheray mais en tres
baief en ces pns passatges aus
quelz elle nappartiet directemt

par ce qlle fut faicte par xpi
ens sur xpiens. En la cite de
Iadres asseigree ou procham
precedent article aduinerent
mahieu de mont morency
et plusieurs autres seigneis
et pelerins francois. Et en
celle mesmes cite bint par
deuers les pelerins Alexis
filz de sursac Iadis empeur

Chalice from the treasury of St Mark's. It is made of sardonyx and silver gilt, adorned with pearls and enamelled medallions. The chalice is one of the 32 that were taken to Venice after the sack of Constantinople by the Fourth Crusade.

Opposite The Crusader fleet and camp in front of the fortifications of Constantinople. From *Les Passages faits Outremer par les Français contre les Turcs et autres Sarrasins et Maures outremarins. c* 1490. Bibliothèque Nationale, Paris

That evening, towards six o'clock, the barons and the Doge of Venice assembled for a conference in a church on the further side of the harbour, close to where they had been encamped. Many different points of view were exchanged at that meeting; the French, in particular, were greatly distressed by the reverse they had suffered that day. Many of those present advised an attack on the city from another side, at a place where the defences were weaker. The Venetians, who had more experience of the sea, pointed out that if they went to that side, the current would carry them down the straits, and they would be unable to stop their ships. There were, I might say, certain people in the company who would have been only too pleased if the current had borne them down the straits, or the wind had done so; they did not care where they went, so long as they left that land behind and went on their way. Nor was that to be wondered at, for we were in very grave danger at the time.

After much discussion, it was finally decided to spend the next day, which was a Saturday, and the whole of Sunday, repairing the damage done to the ships and the equipment, and to renew the assault on the Monday. This time they would have the ships that carried the scaling ladders bound together, two by two, so that each pair could make a combined attack on one tower. This plan was adopted because, in that day's engagement, they had noticed that when only one ship had attacked each tower, the greater number of men on a tower than on a ladder had made it too heavy a task for a ship to undertake alone. It was therefore reasonable to assume that two ships together would do more effective damage than one. This plan of binding the ships in pairs was carried out while the troops were standing by on the Saturday and the Sunday.

Meanwhile the Emperor Murzuphlus had come to encamp with all his forces on an open space directly opposite our lines, and had pitched his scarlet tents there. Thus matters remained till the Monday morning, when all the men on the various ships got their arms and equipment ready. The citizens of Constantinople were now much less afraid of our troops than at the time of our first assault. They were

The marble slab which once covered the grave of Henricus Dandolo in the middle bay of the south gallery of Hagia Sophia. The blind Doge of Venice was one of the leaders of the Fourth Crusade, and was the one chiefly responsible for persuading the Latins to attack Constantinople. Following the conquest of Constantinople, three-eighths of the city was given to him. He died the following year in 1205 and was buried in the south gallery of Hagia Sophia. After about sixty years of Latin occupation the Byzantines managed to reconquer Constantinople. Dandolo's grave was opened and his bones were thrown to the dogs. It is said that even the dogs did not eat his bones!

in fact in such a confident mood that all along the walls and towers there was nothing to be seen but people. Then began a fierce and magnificent assault, as each ship steered a straight course forward. The shouts that rose from the battle created such a din that it seemed as if the whole earth were crumbling to pieces.

The assault had been going on for a considerable time when our Lord raised for us a wind called Boreas, which drove the ships still further on to the shore. Two of the ships which were bound together - one called the 'Pilgrim' and the other the 'Paradise' - approached so close to a tower, one of them on one side and one on the other, as God and the wind drove them onwards, that the ladder of the 'Pilgrim' made contact with it. Immediately a Venetian, in company with the French knight named André Durboise, forced their way in. Other men began to follow them, and in the end the defenders were routed and driven out.

The moment the knights aboard the transports saw this happen, they landed, and raising their ladders against the wall, climbed to the top, and took four more towers. Then all the rest of the troops started to leap out of warships, galleys and transports, helter-skelter, each as fast as he could. They broke down about three of the gates and entered the city. The horses were then taken out of the transports; the knights mounted and rode straight towards the place where the Emperor Murzuphlus had his camp. He had his battalions drawn up in front of the tents; but as soon as his men saw the knights charging towards them on horseback, they retreated in disorder. The Emperor himself fled through the streets of the city to the castle of Bucoleon.

Then followed a scene of massacre and pillage: on every hand the Greeks were cut down, their horses, palfreys, mules and other possessions snatched as booty. So great was the number of killed and wounded that no man could count them. A great part of the Greek nobles had fled towards the gate of Blachernae; but by this time it was past six o'clock, and our men had grown weary of fighting and slaughtering. The troops began to assemble in a great square inside Constantinople. Then, convinced that it would take them at least a month to subdue the whole city, with its great churches and palaces and the people inside it, they decided to settle down near the walls and towers they had already captured...

Our troops, all utterly worn out and weary, rested quietly that night. But the Emperor Murzuphlus did not rest; instead, he assembled his forces and said he was going to attack the Franks. However he did not do as he had announced, but rode along certain streets as far away as possible from those occupied by our army, till he came to a gate called the Golden Gate through which he escaped, and so left the city...

The Marquis de Montferrat rode straight along the shore to the palace of Bucoleon. As soon as he arrived there the palace was surrendered to him, on condition that the lives of all the people in it should be spared... In the same way that the palace of Bucoleon was surrendered to the Marquis de Montferrat, so the palace of Blachernae was yielded to the Comte de Flandre's brother Henri, and on the same conditions. There too was found a great store of treasure, not less than there had been in the palace of Bucoleon... The rest of the army, scattered throughout the city, also gained much booty; so much, indeed, that no one could estimate its amount or its value. It included gold and silver, table-services and precious stones, satin and silk, mantles of squirrel fur, ermine and miniver, and every choicest thing to be found on this earth. Geoffroy de Villehardouin here declares that, to his knowledge, so much booty had never been gained in any city since the creation of the world...

The crusaders paid 50,000 marks to the Venetians and distributed twice this sum among their soldiers who had already become rich with the booty.

The Venetians were the financiers of the crusade, and thus claimed the largest portion of the booty. Much of the treasure carried away by the Crusaders is now in the treasury of St Mark's in Venice.

Among the relics looted by the crusaders were the pieces of the True Cross, and the iron of the lance with which Christ was pierced at his side, two of the nails which were used to nail him on the cross, a crystal phial with his blood, his tunic and the crown of thorns – the last two were carried to France and housed in the specially built St Chapelle in Paris.

The damage done to the Christian city of Constantinople shocked the pope as well as the rest of the Christian world. The Eastern Greek Orthodox world would never forgive the west for what they had done.

The four bronze horses of St Mark's carried away by the Crusaders from Constantinople. Venice

THE FOUR BRONZE HORSES OF ST MARK'S

Among the forces which constituted the Fourth Crusade Venice was the most important maritime power. In April 1203 the Doge of Venice Henricus Dandolo led the Venetian fleet of 200 ships carrying some 25,000 men towards the walls of Constantinople which was then the richest city in the world. Its forums were adorned with monuments brought from various parts of the former Roman empire. The conquerors did not only plunder the privately owned villas or palaces, but shared all sorts of movable objects of art as well. In addition to the art treasures, the Doge acquired three-eighths of the Byzantine empire, the port of Gallipoli, the west coast of Greece and the wealthy city of Adrianople (today's Edirne). Outstanding among the masterpieces acquired by Venice were the four bronze horses which until a few years ago decorated the central entrance of St Mark's Venice. These four gilded bronze horses, which became the most treasured spoils of Dandolo, had once graced the Hippodrome. It is not known whether these horses were produced in Greece or Rhodes or Rome, but they have been carried back and forth across Europe several times, either as spoils of victory or for safekeeping in two world wars.

Until recently, scholarly studies had shown that the horses were apparently of Greek origin. Some attribute them to the fourth century BC, 'Greek work of the time of Alexander or just after'. Some scholars have quoted Pliny's *Naturalis Historia* which mentions a 'quadriga of the Sun made for Rhodes' by Lysippos and claimed that 'this is the quadriga of San Marco'. 20 years ago a German archaeologist believed he had found proof of this theory. In the sanctuary at Delphi he compared markings on a marble base with the position of the St Mark's hooves, and translated an inscription on the pedestal 'To Apollo from the people of Rhodes'. Recent appraisals have been weighted on the side of the theory which favours Roman origin. This theory suggests that the horses were created to adorn a triumphal arch in the waning days of the Roman empire. Technical analyses show the bronze alloy to be about 98 percent pure copper, with one percent each of tin and lead making up the difference. The technical difficulties of casting such an alloy suggest the late Imperial period, and details such as the stylized treatment of ears, hooves and nostrils are comparable with Roman sculptures of the second and third centuries AD, such as the magnificent horse of Marcus Aurelius which stood in Rome. Greek art authorities put forward the theory that they are 'probably a work inspired by a Greek masterpiece from the second half of the fifth century BC'.

When Napoleon subdued Italy in 1799, he had the finest works of art from the peninsula packed up and sent to Paris. From Venice went 20 priceless paintings, 500 manuscripts, the Winged Lion of St Mark's from the Piazzetta and the four horses. The latter were placed on the Arc du Carrousel in 1807 accompanied by two winged victories and a chariot. After Bonaparte's downfall, when the Congress of Vienna re-drew the political map of Europe and established Austrian hegemony over Venice, Emperor Francis I of Austria decreed their return to Italy.

During the two world wars of this century the horses were carted off to safety in Rome in 1917, and to the Benedictine abbey at Praglia in the Euganean hills in 1942. A former director of St Mark's once said that 'Each time these horses are moved, an empire falls' citing ancient Rome, Byzantium, Venice, Napoleon, Austria, Mussolini and the Third Reich as examples, but the world has run out of empires, and now the horses have descended from their loggia for the last time.

In the past 20 years it had become increasingly apparent that they were suffering from bronze disease, a pernicious form of corrosion. Under the gilding some of the rich copper alloy was turning to powder. Eventually holes would appear, legs buckle, details blur and the horses disintegrate; accelerating air pollution was the

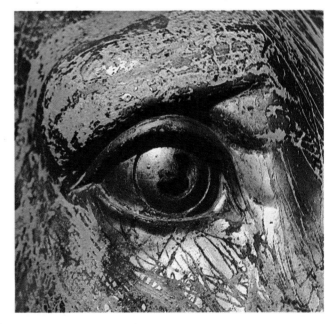

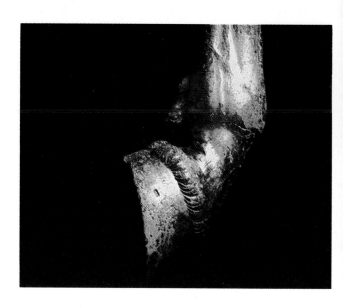

chief culprit. Heavy, chemically saturated, corrosive condensation settled on the horses. Only removal, treatment and relocation indoors could save them.

In 1974 the first horse was lifted down gently and carried to a laboratory inside the basilica for a series of delicate and sophisticated tests. Then treatment began. Damaging chloride and sulphate salts were identified, then corrosive deposits were loosened various chemicals and softly brushed away. Each horse was washed with a surfactant, given a stabilizing alkaline treatment and a final distilled water rinsing. Solutions pumped into its cavities dissolved and flushed dirt, mould and soluble salts from the interior. Gradually, as encrustations and stains were removed, the horse's gilt glowed afresh. During laboratory studies, photogrammetric studies plotted its contours so that a copy could be made without resorting to plaster casts, for facsimiles had to replace the bronze horses of St Mark's façade.

After some 700 years of presiding over the joys and sorrows of Venice from a loggia high on the façade of the Basilica of St Mark's, the four horses have come down to earth, and will now be displayed for citizens and visitors within the Museo Marciano.

Throughout the centuries, Venetian artists like Gentile Bellini, Carpaccio, Canaletto, Francesco Guardi – and many others from other lands, have included the horses in their paintings. Illustrious visitors including Petrarch, Goethe and Stendhal have written about them while Italy's hotel chains have used their emblem on letterheads and menus.

HAGIA SOPHIA AS A MOSQUE

On April 6, 1453 the Ottoman army of Sultan Mehmet II (1451-81) appeared in front of the walls of Constantinople. Until then, since its foundation by Byzas, it had witnessed over 20 sieges and defied most of them – mainly owing to its strong walls reinforced by towers, extending from the coast of the Marmara to the Golden Horn on the land side.

The last Byzantine Emperor Constantine XI Dragazes* knew that the end of his small city-empire was approaching and appealed to the Western Christian world. In answer to the Emperor Constantine's desperate plea the pope sent Cardinal Isidore and 200 soldiers. At the cardinal's first act, which was the promulgation of a Dictium of Union in the great Hagia Sophia, including the name of the pope, the populace is said to have rejected him with the furious cry 'Better the turban of the Turk than the pope's tiara'. The Genoese sent 3,000 troops, and Constantine courageously prepared to do battle, but his army was still totally inadequate to man the walls and repair the breaches.

The entrance to the harbour was blocked by a very strong iron chain of which surviving pieces are at present displayed in İstanbul Archaeological Museums and the Military Museum. However, one morning to their horror the Byzantines saw over 70 Turkish war vessels in front of their walls in the Golden Horn. The Ottomans had built a road of planks over the hills of Pera and transported their men-of-war on greased rafts from the Bosphorus into the harbour. This was a severe shock to the defence and morale of the Byzantines.

The Ottoman siege lasted for about seven weeks, and after a period of 1123 years the Christian history of the city of Constantinople came to an end. On May 29th, 1453 the 21 year old Ottoman Sultan Mehmet II captured the city. In late afternoon, when order was somewhat established, he rode through the streets of Constantinople to Hagia Sophia escorted by his ministers. Entering the church, he stood still for some moments, gazing silently before him, then he walked towards the altar. As he did so he noticed a soldier hacking at a piece of marble pavement. The sultan turned on him, demanding to know why he was destroying the floor. The soldier answered 'In the name of the Faith'. Enraged, Mehmet II struck the soldier with his sword, exclaiming, 'For you the treasure and prisoners are enough, the buildings of the city fall to me.' According to the Christian historian Ducas, 'the soldier was dragged by the feet and thrown outside, half dead'.

* The legends about the end of the last Byzantine emperor are numerous. Most of them agree that he died fighting. His grave has not been located.

Interior of Hagia Sophia by Chevalier Gaspare Fossati in the middle of the nineteenth century

Opposite Imaginary miniature of the siege of Constantinople in 1453. From *The Voyage across the Seas* by Bertrandon de la Broquière. Second half of the fifteenth century. Bibliothèque Nationale, Paris. Despite the ignorance of the artists of such details as the garments of Ottoman soldiers or the architecture of Hagia Sophia, the famous artillery of the Ottomans and the method by which their warships were transported overland from the Bosphorus as well as the barrel bridge that linked the Turkish forces on both sides of the inlet, are clearly seen.

According to the Islamic tradition once the Prophet Mohammed, saying 'They will conquer Constantinople. Hail to the Prince and the army to whom this will be granted', prophesied that one day the city would be conquered by Muslims. Although the various attempts of Arab forces in the seventh century and of several Ottoman sultans before him had failed Mehmet the Conquerer now fulfilled this prophecy. As for Constantine the Great erecting a monument as great as Hagia Sophia signified the victory of Christianity over paganism, for Mehmet II the Conqueror transforming it into a mosque meant the victory of Islam over Christianity. The sultan gave orders that the Great Church be turned into a mosque. It is said that the devastation that the Fourth Crusade caused in Constantinople was so great that when the city fell to the Turks Hagia Sophia did not have money to buy candles. The large metal cross that crowned the summit of the dome was immediately replaced by a crescent. The ambo, thrones, altar, icons and relics and the bells from its belltower were removed. A pulpit or *minber* in place of the ambo, and a *mihrap*, or prayer niche, in the curve of the sanctuary apse, to direct the Moslem believers towards Mecca, were built. However, since Mecca does not fall to the east but somewhat south-east from İstanbul, the niche had to be placed obliquely. The first two minarets were also added by Mehmet II. After this date for 482 years and until it was turned into a museum in 1935, by the orders of Atatürk, the founder of modern Turkey, the edifice would serve as a mosque for Moslem believers and an example for a large number of Ottoman architects. The enormous candlesticks

which flank the niche are later additions brought from Hungary (from the cathedral of Buda) by Süleyman the Magnificent. The inscriptions on them praise Sultan Süleyman and Islam.

In accordance with the ban on figures in Islam, the mosaics on the lower walls were plastered over. However, since the name of the church was understood as the 'House of Worship (*ibadetgah*) of God' it would continue to be used in the form of *Ayasofya*.

The ancient literary sources indicate that the mosaic of the Pantokrator which occupied the dome was plastered over during the reign of Ahmet I (1603-17) and the Virgin and Christ Child and the flanking archangels in the reign of Mahmut I (1730-54). Meanwhile Selim II (1566-74) had rebuilt one of the minarets and Murat III (1574-95) had added two more minarets.

By the nineteenth century although extensive repair work was done during the reign of Selim II by Sinan, natural disasters had made the restoration of Hagia Sophia imperative. In 1846 Sultan Abdül Mecit commissioned two Swiss architects, Gaspare and Guisseppe Fossati, to undertake the monumental assignment. After working for more than two years the Fossatis completed the restoration of the building. In addition to strengthening the dome and vaults and heightening the south-eastern minaret to the level of the other three, the mosaics were uncovered, cleaned, and covered with plaster. However, the four seraphim on the pendentives were left opened but with star medallions added to their faces. The ultimate total cost of the extensive restoration work is said to have amounted to some US $ 2,000,000 and was financed by the legacy of a childless sheikh. The rectangular medallions on the piers were replaced by larger round ones during the restoration. The four on the main piers carry the names of the First Four Caliphs of Islam, and those on the western secondary piers give the names of the grandsons of Mohammed. Beginning with the one in the picture, anti-clockwise they read Allah, Mohammed, Ömer, Ali, Hüseyin, Hasan, Osman and Ebu Bekir.

After it became a mosque the gardens to the south of Hagia Sophia were used for *türbes* or royal sepulchres of various sultans and the members of their families. The oldest of these buildings is the *türbe* of Mustafa I and İbrahim, and was originally the baptistery of the church. The other imperial *türbes* belong to Sultans Selim II, Murat III and Mehmet III (1595-1603). In addition to tombs of the sultans, the *türbes* also house those of their wives and close relatives. Among the three most important *türbes* is that of Sultan Selim II. It is the work of the great Ottoman architect, Sinan, and it contains superb tiles from İznik (Nicaea).

Some of the old legends about the edifice have lingered to the present day. Among its columns none can challenge the one located in the north-western exedra of the church in popularity. This is commonly known as the column of St Gregory the Miracle Worker. A tradition claims that under this column a cistern existed and the dampness of water could be felt on the surface of the column, thus causing it to be named as the 'sweating' (or according to more polite tour guides 'perspiring') column. It is said that one day Justinian the Great had been running around with a splitting headache: neither the number of aspirin or bufferin tablets he swal-

Pages 40,41 and 42 Fossati engravings showing the environs and interior of the third Hagia Sophia in the middle of the nineteenth century.

43

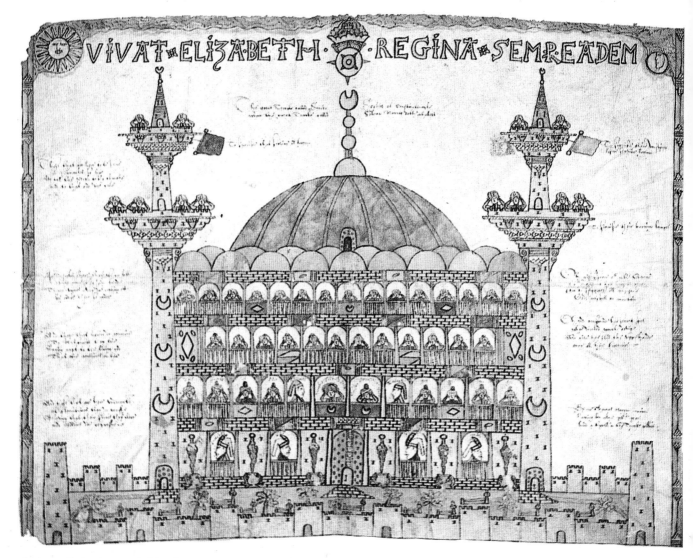

VIVAT ELIZABETH REGINA SEMPEADEM

A fanciful view of Hagia Sophia by an Englishman taken prisoner by the Turks during the reign of Queen Elizabeth I (1596-1662). British Library, London.

Opposite Interior decoration of Hagia Sophia after the Iconoclasm (after E. M. Antoniades)

lowed nor his prayers were able to help. As he was walking by this column he rested his head on its cool surface and immediately his headache disappeared. After this miracle, the superstitious Byzantines started to touch the column when they suffered from hangovers and gradually a hole came into existence. As the size of the hole and the number of believers wearing away the column increased, its healing powers increased as well. At the time these lines were being written, touching this hole (no matter which finger one puts into it or how long he keeps it there) was known to be a remedy for hangovers; in addition to this, it was a nostrum of fertility for those women who failed to become pregnant. It is also said that one should look at the tip of his finger after putting it into the hole; the damper it is, the better his character. Similar holes with magical curing powers are often encountered in the ancient Greek world.

The two beautiful marble ablution urns located in Hagia Sophia are said to be Hellenistic but were installed here by Sultan Murat III. Tradition has it that they were unearthed, full of gold, with another, by a peasant plowing near Pergamum. The peasant promptly reburied them and rushed to the capital to relate his discovery to the sultan. On the sultan's orders, two of the urns were removed and the third was presented to the peasant. Before accepting it, he required it to be emptied, explaining to the vizier, 'Our sultan gave me the urn, he said nothing about the gold it contained'. As a further reward for his honesty the peasant was presented with the field in which the urns were found.

MOSAICS

It has been suggested that the original decoration of Hagia Sophia probably did not include figured mosaics, and several reasons have been claimed in support of this idea. One of these was that the artists of the original decorations did not find such a vast interior suitable for figured mosaics which could not be seen by the onlooker clearly and thus result in the desired effect. The exclusion of figured mosaics may have been a deliberate choice of Justinian in order not to offend the religious factions that were against images. Also the art of mosaic making is a time-taking job and because of the desire to finish and dedicate the building as quickly as possible non-figured mosaic decoration was preferred.

One of the striking features of the interior decoration was the lavish use of gold tesserae – glass mosaic cubes covered with gold. It has been estimated that the golden surface of the various vaults, walls, and the dome contains about 150,000,000 mosaic cubes, using some one thousand tons of glass. In order to match the opaque and polished look of the golden tesserae placed on the flat surface of the walls at the line of sight of the onlooker, the tesserae covering the higher surface were set at an angle towards the bottom or obliquely to catch the light and direct it to other surfaces. This technique of angled tesserae is thought to have been first used in the Church of St Polyeuktos in Constantinople, built 525-27, and it enabled the illumination to reach the dim or poorly lit surfaces of the interior.

Even if there were some panels with figures among the original mosaics of the edifice they must have been destroyed during the period of the Iconoclasm which lasted from 726 to 843. The original non-figured decoration of the building survived the Iconoclasm – and has even reached the present in pristine condition in a very large portion of the vaults and wall surface. However, if there had been images made during this period, or introduced following Justinian's reign, these must have been destroyed or tampered with by the Iconoclasts. Immediately after the restoration of the images in 843, new mosaics such as the Virgin – in the conch of the apse – and the flanking archangels were made. The large side walls of the nave were also said to have been covered with figures of saints. It is thought that a figure of Christ Pantokrator occupied the central dome.

Some of the original non-figured mosaic decoration of the church has survived to the present – though much of it still under the Ottoman or Fossati plaster. The loss of the original mosaics in the galleries and at the higher levels is caused by the loosening of the setting-beds as a result of water seepage, mostly on flat surfaces. Despite the Moslem ban on images, except for the mosaic of Christ Pantokrator at the dome and the tympanum mosaics all the mosaics of the building stood intact until the late seventeenth and early eighteenth centuries.

In the nineteenth century, during their restoration, the Fossati brothers uncovered many mosaics but in deference to Moslem custom they covered them again with whitewash and stencils. In 1931 Thomas Whittemore of the Princeton Institute of Arts started to uncover and restore these.

MOSAIC PANELS
(NAVE AND NARTHEX)

Christ and the Emperor Leo VI the Wise (886-912) (page 48-49)
Late ninth century. Lunette of the Imperial Door

In the Greek Orthodox churches, portraying the patron saint of the church above the main entrance was a custom and the location of this mosaic confirms this custom. At its centre, Christ is represented enthroned. In His left hand the Book of Gospels is seen. The inscription in Greek reads *Peace be with you. I am the light of the world*. His hands and feet are disproportionately large as compared with His head. The medallions which flank Him show the Virgin and the archangel Gabriel. In front of Him and on the ground there is a monarch, the Emperor Leo VI the Wise humbling himself before his suzerian, and thus the panel is interpreted as defining the Byzantine empire, governed by Christ through His vice regent on earth, the emperor.

The emperor is seen with his hands raised in a pose of supplication. His eyes are turned away from the majesty before him in concentrated meditation. He is nimbate. This marks him as a terrestrial monarch. Christ's nimbus is that of the King of Heaven.

Tradition has it that the emperor as seen in the panel might be pleading with Christ to forgive him for the frequency of his nuptials. For he had lost three wives without producing a male heir, and wished to take a fourth mate, ordinarily forbidden by the Orthodox Church. He finally obtained permission to marry his mistress, Zoe, and legitimized his bastard son.

In comparison with the importance of the place assigned to it, the mosaic shows poor workmanship, probably due to the scarcity of skilful mosaic makers at the time it was made which was the result of the Iconoclasm. The figures are bulky. All of them have broad faces, big broad noses and large eyes. However, the inclination of the individual tesserae from the vertical plane deserves emphasis. Here, the observer is at a distance of 10.1 m from the mosaic which is placed at a height of 9.8 m. The inclination of the individual tesserae is 30°, indicating an attempt to place the mosaic at right angles to the line of the beholder. This panel as well those of the Virgin and Christ Child in the bema of the apse and the flanking archangels remained visible till the mid–eighteenth century.

The Virgin and Christ Child (page 50)
Ninth century. Conch of the apse

This is the earliest of the figured mosaics in Hagia Sophia and dates to the period immediately after the Iconoclasm. The Virgin is represented seated on pillows placed on a jewelled throne, and holding the Christ Child. Both figures are nimbate.

Archangel Gabriel (page 51)
Tenth century. Southern end of the arch which frames the conch of the apse

The archangel Michael is represented standing, and holding a sceptre in his right hand and a globe in the other hand. From the figure of Gabriel which was opposite Michael only fragments remain.

The Virgin between Justinian and Constantine. Late tenth century. Hagia Sophia. Lunette of the vestibule gate

The Virgin between Justinian and Constantine
Late tenth century. Lunette of the vestibule gate

In the mosaic, the protector of Church and State, the Virgin, accepts a model of the church from Justinian and a model of the city of Constantinople from Constantine. In other words, it shows the two monarchs who fulfill their duties to Church and State. Justinian the Great is assimilated to the saints. The inscription at his back reads *Justinian, Emperor of illustrious memory*. Constantine the Great is officially canonized though he received baptism just before dying. The inscription at his back reads *Constantine, the Great Emperor amongst the Saints*.

The inscription which is divided into two by the Virgin's head reads: *Theotokos*, or 'the Mother of God'. The appearance, disposition and colour of the dress of the Virgin give the impression that the garment is made of heavy, soft, lustrous silk stained with the imperial purple. Her feet are set on a stool. On the top of the stool

silver mosaic was used and so closely set, like a single plate of burnished silver, as to give the impression that the Mother of God rests her feet not on a simple footstool but on a piece of white cloud.

Constantine the Great offers to the Mother of God and to Christ Child the city of Constantinople, the model town-symbol similar to many conventional representations of cities in early Christian art. The two basilica-shaped buildings within the walls may represent symbolically two of its monuments, one the first basilica of Hagia Sophia said to have been erected at the time of Constantine and the other the senate.

MOSAIC PANELS (GALLERIES)

During the early history of the building the entire gallery was used as the women's quarter. In later centuries most of the south gallery was reserved for the use of the royal family so that they were able to perform their religious duties without being seen by the crowd in the nave. In addition to this the meetings of high clergy were held here. For these reasons it is natural to come across some of the most important mosaic panels in this section of the church.

The date and purpose of the marble screen in the south gallery is not known. It is not an original part of the church but a later addition. It is made in the form of two pairs of false double doors with elaborately ornamented panels, the so-called Gates of Heaven and Hell.

Hagia Sophia. Stone-paved north-west ramp to the galleries

Opposite Christ from the Deesis. South gallery – middle bay

Page 58 The Virgin from the Deesis. South gallery – middle bay

Page 59 Saint John the Baptist from the Deesis. South gallery – middle bay

The Deesis
Second half of the thirteenth or the first half of the fourteenth centuries. South gallery – middle bay

Deesis is the iconographic name used for the scene where Christ is portrayed between the Virgin and St John the Baptist. In the mosaic the last two are seen interceding on behalf of humanity. They lean toward Christ in suppliant attitudes, pleading, so the iconographers interpret, for the salvation of mankind. St John looks toward Christ with an expression of almost agonized grief on his face. His total expression is of humble devotion to the figure in front of him. The Virgin casts her gaze shyly downwards. Her expression is of tender serenity. A spirit of humanity lights up the features of both the Virgin and Saint John, portrayed with a subtlety rarely achieved in mosaic. At the centre, Christ is seen sitting on a throne which has not survived. From the footstool on which His feet must have rested only a few mosaics are left. He holds His right hand in a gesture of benediction. His left hand rests on a gospel whose cover is jewelled. He looks into space with an expression of sadness in His eyes, appearing here as if He has more of the nature of man than of God.

This mosaic is referred to as one of the greatest works and triumphs of mosaic art in Constantinople. It is the illustration of the cultural revival which took place in the capital after the restoration of the Byzantine empire by Michael Palaiologos in 1261. The scholars do not agree on its exact date. While some date it to the second half of the thirteenth century, there are those who date it to the beginning of the fourteenth. About two-thirds of the mosaic has vanished, but the features of the three figures are still completely intact and unmarred. They are studies in refinement and pathos.

56

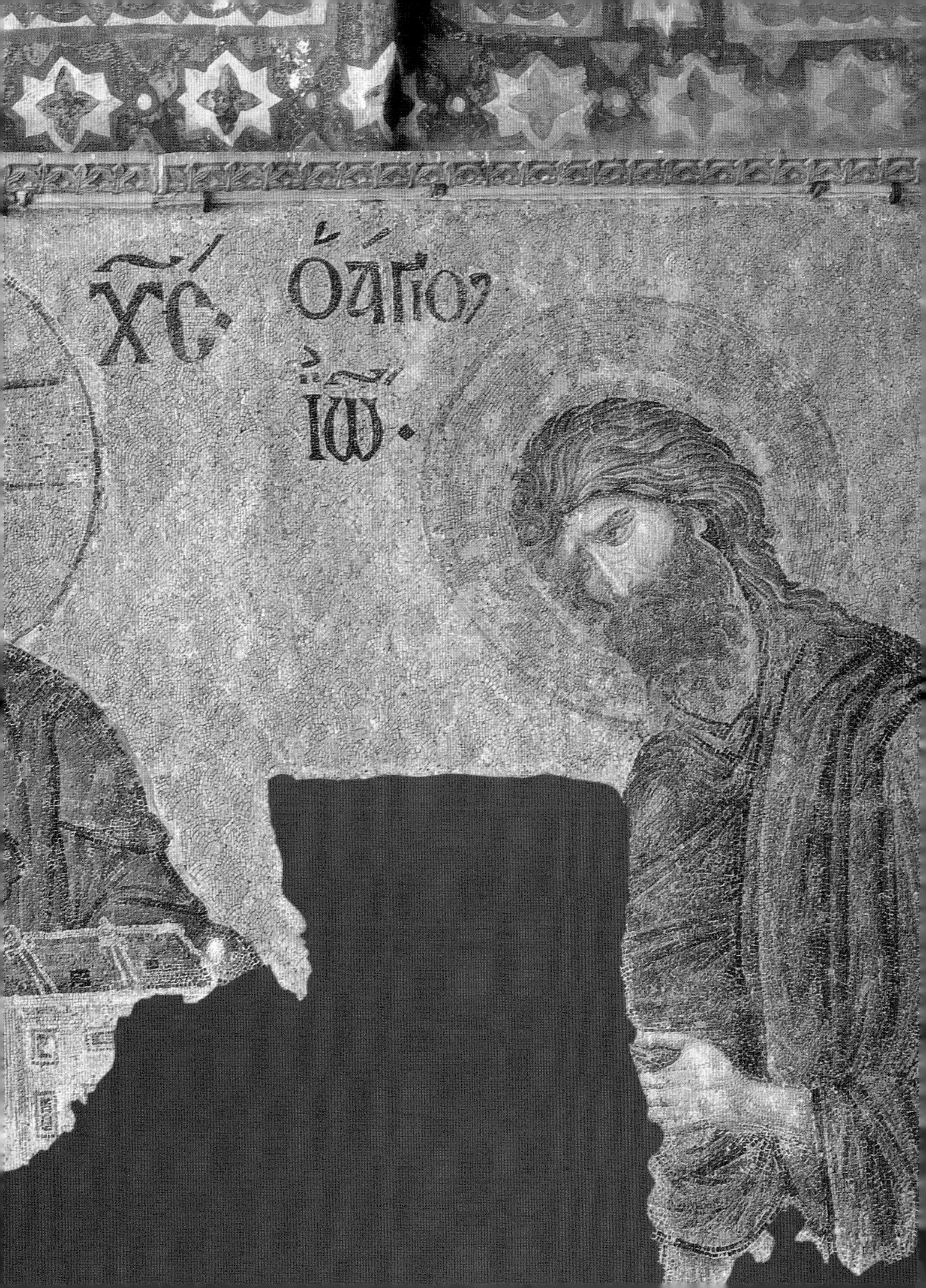
XC
Ο ΑΓΙΟC
ΙΩ

Christ Pantokrator, the Empress Zoe and the Emperor Constantine IX Monomachos

Mid–eleventh and early twelfth centuries. South gallery – last bay. Two monarchs are seen in the act of offering Christ symbolic donations – a purse of silver and a scroll of privileges. The inscription behind the emperor reads *Constantine in Christ the God, Autocrat, faithful King of the Romans, Monomakos*. The inscription designates the Empress Zoe as *the most pious Augusta*. The inscription on the scroll held by her reads *Constantine in Christ the God, faithful King of the Romans, Monomakos*.

In this mosaic only the heads of the three figures and those parts of the inscriptions bearing Constantine's name can be assigned to their reign. Zoe (1028-50) was successively married to three basileis: Romanus III (1028-34), Michael IV (1034-41) and Constantine IX Monomachos (1042-55). It seems that when she married the latter, her new husband's head replaced the previous one. It appears that the same thing had been done when she had married her second husband. However, not only the head of Zoe and her husbands but the head of Christ as well were remade when the couple succeeded to the throne. It is probable that during his brief reign Michael V (1041-42) destroyed the faces of his enemies, Zoe and Michael IV, but he would not have interfered with Christ. When the heads were made, the artist did not find it suitable to have incongruous pictorial elements within the same panel and so remade the head of Christ; an act demonstrating the aesthetic sensibilities of the artist.

The Virgin and Christ Child, the Emperor John II Komnenos and the Empress Irene. Twelfth century. South gallery – last bay. This panel may almost certainly be dated to 1118, the year of the coronation of John II Komnenos (1118-43) and his wife Irene. It was a little later that Alexios, their son, was also given a place on a nearby section of wall. Slightly taller than the others, the figure of the Virgin forms the central axis. Her title reads *Mother of God*. Her figure is strongly indicated in dark blue. Her face is grave but strangely young. It reminds one of the face of the Virgin such as seen in the best icons. The dresses of the imperial figures are enamelled with pearls and precious

stones, giving an appearance of coats of mail. With such sumptuous costumes no extra emphasis is needed to bring out the lines of the bodies. Only the faces between crown and necklets are visible. The tendency to widen faces gives them a slightly Mongolian air.

The emperor is seen offering a bag of gold. The inscription reads, *John, in Christ the God faithful King born in the purple and Autocrat of the Romans, Komnenos.*

The redhaired empress is seen holding a scroll. The accompanying inscription reads *Irene the most pious Augusta.*

CHRONOLOGY OF HAGIA SOPHIA

360 Constantius II builds or dedicates first church of Hagia Sophia.

404 Fire destroys roof of Hagia Sophia

414 Second fire ravages Hagia Sophia

415 Rebuilt church dedicated by Theodosius II

532 Hagia Sophia burned to ground during Victory Riots and the construction of the third church begun

537 Justinian consecrates rebuilt Hagia Sophia

553 Earthquake weakens crown of eastern arch; Justinian summons church council in Hagia Sophia to reconcile Monophysites

557 Second earthquake splits arch

558 Eastern arch and part of main dome collapse

563 Restored church reconsecrated

725 Leo III, the Isaurian issues his first edict against image worship.

726-843 Iconoclasm (interrupted 780–813)

741 A great earthquake

865 Erection of a belfry near the west front of the church

869 Earthquakes. The vaulting cracks in several places. Earthquake damages western half of dome

869-70 The Eighth Ecumenical Council is held in Hagia Sophia.

c 875 Basil I, the Macedonian consolidates the great arch to the west by an additional thickness.

876 Redecoration of Hagia Sophia begun; figured mosaics introduced

886-912 Reign of Leo VI – mosaic in the inner narthex of Hagia Sophia

975 Western arch totters and falls dragging the dome with it in an earthquake.

981 Basil II restores the building.

987 The ambassadors of Vladimir dazzled by the grandeur of the divine service in Hagia Sophia, decide on the conversion of Russia to the Orthodox Greek Church.

989 Earthquake brings down Hagia Sophia's western arch and semidome

1042-55 Reign of Constantine IX, Monomachos; mosaic in the last bay of the southern gallery of Hagia Sophia

1054 The envoys of Pope Leo IX excommunicate the Eastern Church in Hagia Sophia

1203 Crusaders arrive in Constantinople; Alexios III flees; Crusaders restore Isaac II to the throne; he and this son Alexios IV were crowned in Hagia Sophia as co-emperors

1204-61 Lascarid dynasty in Nicaea

1261 Greeks recapture Constantinople and restore Byzantine empire; Michael VIII founder of the Palaiologos, was crowned emperor in Hagia Sophia which is restored to the Orthodox faith.

1317 Andronicus II, Palaiologos, the Elder, adds pyramidal tower-buttresses disfiguring the exterior.

1344 Serious earthquake damages Hagia Sophia

1346 Eastern arch and part of the dome collapse in earthquakes

1346-56 Major restoration undertaken

1391 Coronation of Manuel II Palaiologos in Hagia Sophia

1452 Act of Union with Rome celebrated in Hagia Sophia. Te Deum is again sung in the church by the order of the last Byzantine Emperor Constantine XI Palaiologos.

1453 Fall of Constantinople. Hagia Sophia converted into a mosque and consecrated to Moslem worship

1566-74 Reign of Selim II, who rebuilds the minaret at north-west corner of the mosque

1573 Sinan adds new supporting buttresses to Hagia Sophia

1574-95 Reign of Murat III, who adds two more minarets

1623-40 Reign of Murat IV, who commissions railed balconies for interior of mosque

1703-30 Reign of Ahmet III, builder of a new sultan's box

c 1750 Interior mosaics obscured with whitewash

1766 Earthquakes damage Hagia Sophia

1847 Full restoration of Hagia Sophia begun by Swiss architects Gaspare and Giuseppe Fossati during reign of Abdul Mecit.

1849 Restored Hagia Sophia inaugurated

1894 Earthquake damages interior decoration and restoration by Abdul Hamit II.

1923 Foundation of the Turkish Republic

1932 Work begun on restoration of mosaics

1935 Hagia Sophia reopened as a secular museum

1967 Pope Paul pays official visit to Hagia Sophia

1990 New restoration work begins.